The Professor of Etiquette

A guide to the do's and don'ts of civilized living
with an additional section on the toothpick

Oscar de Mejo

Philomel Books · New York

Library of Congress Cataloging-in-Publication Data De Mejo, Oscar. The professor of
etiquette / written and illustrated by Oscar de Mejo. p. cm. Summary: Pompilius
McGrath, the Professor of Etiquette, gives a lecture in which he identifies various social
blunders and defends the much misunderstood toothpick. ISBN 0-399-21866-1
[1. Etiquette—Fiction. 2. Toothpicks—Fiction. 3. Humorous stories.] I. Title.
PZ7.D3396Pr 1992 [E]—dc20 91-31151 CIP

1 3 5 7 9 10 8 6 4 2
First Impression

$\mathcal{T}$he Professor of Etiquette appeared on the New York scene on a Friday afternoon late that spring. He was first observed tying his shoelaces at the corner of Fifth Avenue and 50th Street, right across from Saks. He had an air of a man mysteriously taken away from a past era and brought lock, stock, and barrel to the present time. When first interviewed, he said that his name was Pompilius McGrath and that he was of Scottish extraction. "I'm a Professor of Etiquette," he said and presented his calling card.

People, of course, remembered the great professor from the time he had lectured in the city a few years back. Now they were looking forward to an announcement of a new lecture. And, sure enough, one day a very conspicuous poster appeared. It announced that Pompilius McGrath, Professor of Etiquette, was giving an important lecture at Madison Square Garden. The lecture was titled THE TOOTHPICK, THIS MISUNDERSTOOD LITTLE FRIEND.

Would a toothpick have the power of packing them in? Indeed I wondered. But on that afternoon of the lecture, Satin Forum was sold out—standing room only. What follows is Prof McGrath's lecture.

"The aim of the lecture," said Prof McGrath, "is to make people understand that in this world of ours it is better to have a well-mannered refined society than individuals who make un-aesthetic faux pas.

"I'm glad that so many children are present because it will mean that we'll have a better society tomorrow."

"Bravo!" shouted several voices from the audience.

"—So," continued the professor, "let me start to present some of the no-nos of human behavior. Here's the first one:

Yawning in public
without covering your mouth—ugly.

Leaving on the train all the
garbage you have produced while traveling.

Gesticulating in the street while
describing some imaginary earthquake scene,
with the danger of hitting some passerby
smack in the face.

Stepping in or out of the elevator
before the ladies, actually jumping in front
of them callously thinking that you've got
to be the first in or out.

Talking loudly at a benefit
performance with no respect for either
performers or nearby patrons.

Circulating in the streets of the big city
with gigantic bundles and bags, hitting people
right and left with the utmost nonchalance
and not one word of apology.

Sneezing explosively without
covering your nose, letting your germs infect
people around you. On the next page we have
a close-up of these germs.

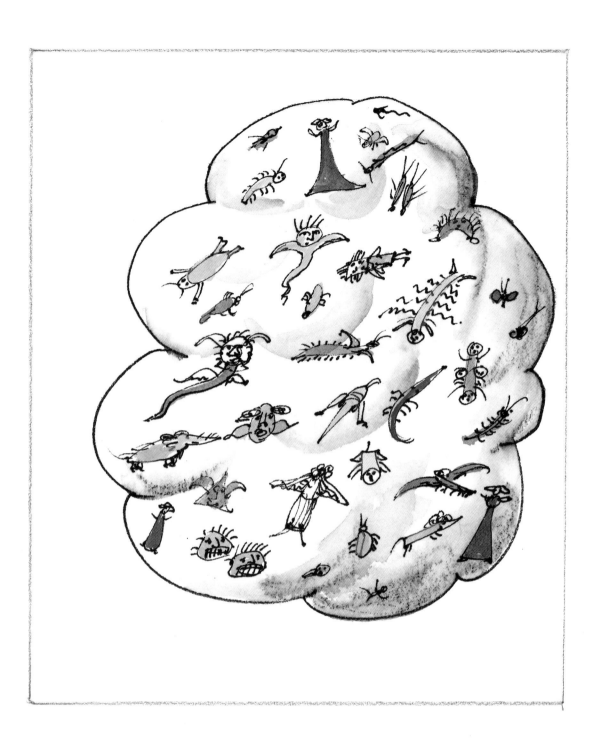

Germs of a cold from a sneeze
floating in the air (magnified 60,000 times).
Not a very pretty sight.
No sir.

Raising your voice ad infinitum
in a coffee shop or restaurant and broadcasting
inconsequential bits of news to the remotest
corners of the place.

Blowing your nose in a
paper or cloth napkin and leaving it
on the restaurant table after your meal.
A revolting faux pas.

Putting large
pieces of food in your mouth.

Cutting meat by holding
the fork in your fist as butchers do.

Eating peas by placing them on a knife
and running the knife across your mouth.
Dangerous aside from ugly.

Drinking milk or tea
with little finger of your hand raised—
a pathetic affectation.

Eating spaghetti with fork and spoon
and believing it to be terribly Italian.
Italians never use fork and spoon, they use
the side of the dish to roll the
spaghetti on the fork.

Keeping arms glued to the table,
bringing mouth to food or drink rather than
food or drink to mouth.

Finishing soup by letting it
drip in your mouth from the plate.

Using the nail of your little finger
to remove food from between your teeth."

A thunderous ovation followed and Professor McGrath had to bow many times. Then he raised his hand, and when silence was restored he said, "You have a half-hour intermission during which time you will be served some steak and a toothpick. It's important that you eat, since this will be part of my lecture, but don't use the toothpick."

He bowed once more then disappeared in the darkness of the backstage.

When the curtain went up, the professor appeared in the center of the stage, sitting at a table, in the process of eating a steak.

Then he stood up and in the tense silence of the audience he said, "Here we are now, you and I, both after a meal of steak. Are we comfortable? Well, I am. You? I doubt it—and how could you be, with all those particles of meat between your teeth—"

He smiled. "Do you see any between mine? There's one reason and one reason only why my teeth are clean!" The suspense in the audience was mounting.

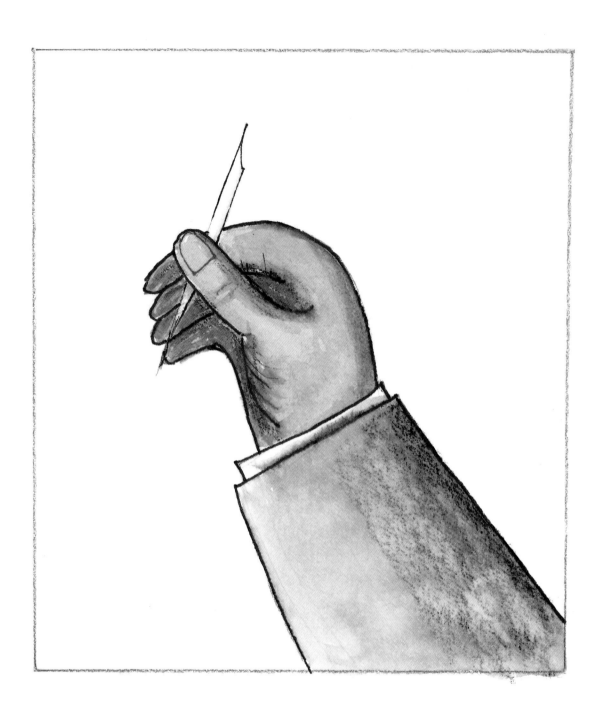

"Here it is!" He showed what he was holding. "It's the tooth-pick, this misunderstood little friend. I used it discreetly at the end of my meal and you didn't even notice it."

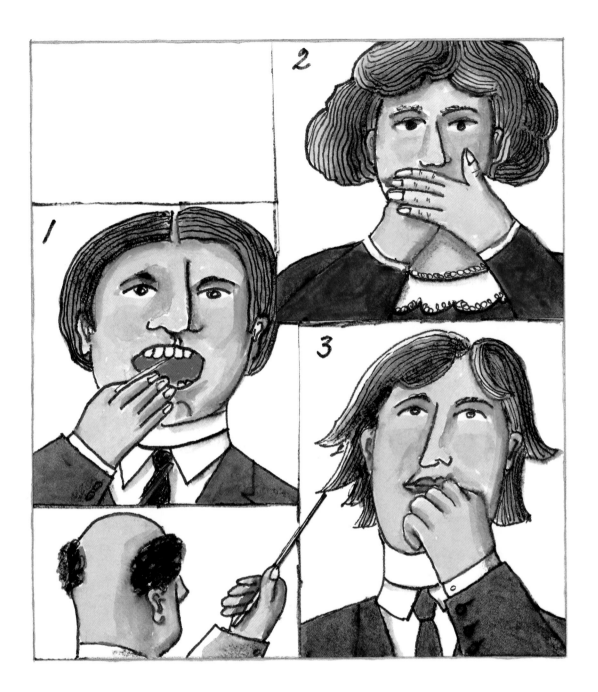

The professor took up his stick and pointed to a board which displayed three images. "The first image," he said, "shows you how not to use your toothpick—too blatant. The second also shows a no-no. There is no necessity to make a screen of one hand to cover the other holding the toothpick. This is like broadcasting the fact that you are using a toothpick. Now, the third image shows the way to do it. Completely casual, with the utmost nonchalance. If you do it discreetly no one will notice it.

"Now before you use your toothpick, let me remind you that you will have to practice a bit before you reach perfection. Don't be discouraged, just do the best you can. And now—go to it!"

The lights went out and in the silence which followed one could hear a faint sound throughout the theater as the audience members were busy with their toothpicks. When the lights came on again, the professor smiled and prepared to resume his talk. After asking the audience how they felt *now* and receiving a thunderous applause of appreciation, the lecture came to its conclusion.

The fifteen minutes that followed were dedicated to an erudite albeit condensed history of the toothpick. Nothing was forgotten. Not Ramses the Second and his two slaves in charge of the Pharaoh's toothpicks, not Nero and the use of the little instrument at his orgiastic banquets. Pompeii was mentioned, and Nineveh, then Athens and the Greek colonies in Sicily. Charlemagne was reported not using toothpicks (the audience booed) but following rulers of the Carolingian Empire apparently had reinstated the use of the tiny instrument at their tables.

The ending of the lecture was a triumph and Professor Pompilius McGrath was raised on the shoulders of a group of men and brought around to the aisles of the theater to shake hands with his friends.

The next day, New York's most prestigious newspaper gave the lecture a headline story to the relief of all its readers, who for years had sacrificed their comfort to the mistaken belief that the toothpick meant bad manners.

After his lecture at the Satin Forum the great man vanished. His fans were dismayed, but his humbleness is to be commended.

He was next observed in Los Angeles at a famous intersection, tying one of his shoelaces. As to his future lectures, no one knows at the present time where they are going to be held. It is indeed difficult, if not impossible, to keep up with the elusive professor and his inseparable little friend, the glorious toothpick.